Nakedness of the Moon

Cosmic Reflections and Poetry

Forrest Knapp

©2020 Forrest Knapp

All rights reserved. No part of this book may be reproduced or used in any manner without the prior written permission of the copyright owner, except for the use of brief quotations in a book review. Photos are licensed from stock photo companies noted, or from the personal collection of the author.

Paperback: 978-1-7360434-1-7
Kindle: 978-1-7360434-2-4

Library of Congress Cataloging Number file with the publisher.

Production by Concierge Publishing Services

Printed in the USA
www.forrestknapp.com

10 9 8 7 6 5 4 3 2 1

For Abby

Photo Credits:

Page		Courtesy of:
	Cover	Pixabay
	Title Page	Pixabay
1	Intro/Who are we?	Denis Belitsky/Shutterstock
2	We Are…	Pixabay
3	Journey of an Oak Leaf	Erkki Makkonen/Shutterstock
4	Path of Heart	Pixabay
5	Gathering Courage	Mike McMahon
6	Nakedness of the Moon	Pixabay
7	Nature's Language	Christian Lagerek/Shutterstock
8	Butterfly Poetry	Jennifer Murray/Pexels
9	Nakedness of the Moon	Pixabay
10	Sacred Path	Vadim Sadovski/Shutterstock
11	The Moon Blushes	kdshutterman/Shutterstock
12	Unfolding Moments	Virginia Allain/Pixabay
13	Appreciation	Vaclav Volrab/Shutterstock
14	Free as a Bird	kwest/Shutterstock
15	Hotel California	Josh Hild/Pexels
16	Enemy of the People	Kaique Rocha/Pexels
17	Unliving the Dream	Pixabay
18	Love What Is	Arm001/Shutterstock
19	Rick's Story	Pixabay
20	Just Be	Pixabay
21	Breathing World Peace	Aron Visuals/Pexels
22	First Class?	Yogendra Singh/Pexels
23	Live Fully within Each New Moment	Vaclav Volrab/Shutterstock
24	Sayeth the Fish	Pixabay
25	Happiness is a Pre-Existing Condition	Pixabay
26	The Manner of Zen	Aleksey Kuprikov/Pexels
27	What Lies Beneath?	Max/Pexels
28	Spirituality vs. Religion	Aleksey Kuprikov/Pexels
29	Beginner's Mind	Tatiana Syrikova/Pexels
30	Willing to Change	Tristan Pokornyi/Pexels
31	Heaven, Purgatory, Hell	Stein Egil Liland/Pexels
32	Far-Away Galaxies	Pixabay
33	Like Judging a Star	Matheus Bertelli/Pexels
34	Engaged in a Mystery	Vadim Sadovski/Shutterstock
35	Look! There We Are…	Pixabay
36	The Puzzle	Eberhard Grossgasteiger/Pexels
37	Universal Perspective	Aleksey Kuprikov/Pexels
38	Looking to the Moon	Frank Cone/Pexels
39	The End is Beautiful	eberhard grossgasteiger/Pexels
40	Earth Appreciation	Pixabay
41	Acknowledgements	Pixabay
	Back Cover	Christian Lagerek/Shutterstock

The purpose of this book is not to provide you with any answers, but rather to inspire you to reflect on the questions. Important questions that are uniquely relevant to the human experience we are having.

What is the nature of our relationship to each other and with the Universe?

Or just...
Who Are We?

We Are...

That crisp sound of rustling leaves on a winter night, the trembling first step of a moment-old kitten.

The unspoken word of an ancient prophet, a lingering memory of freedom.

We are all places at all times within life of all variety and persuasion.

An integral function of the limitless equation - without beginning, without end.

We are all form of all measure within all that one day will become.

We are in all things. Look! There we are...

Journey of an Oak Leaf...

An autumn oak leaf ripens and falls gently
into a stream,

and drifts along current into unfolding
mystery.

It is a journey without beginning
or end, as the stream
will circle and flow
into itself,
again and again.

At home in the oak tree,
at home in the stream,

this journey of an oak leaf lasts
forever it will seem.

For again and again,

it will fall from the oak tree

to become a leaf in the stream.

Path of Heart

Songbirds speak of a path so brightly afront us we can barely hear it. It has been weathered smooth by the aspiration of timeless visionaries.

Where is this path? It slips away within the sound made by seeking for it. It can only be looked upon through clear lens of heart.

The path is a tool for experiencing life. It becomes, itself, the true heart of experience.

You were always meant to walk the path this way, through the steaming rubble of one thousand joys and sorrows. It is a good path.

People often say 'what comes around goes around'. And then we dip our toes just barely into the stream of authentic living. This stream trickles softly, speaking only the language of heart.

A Mindful Life Envelops the Lives of Others.

It takes courage to gaze directly and care deeply about what we see. Compassion is a fundamental activity of our true nature. To be integral of this world is to be wholeheartedly engaged within it.

Meditation is a Method of gathering Courage to practice Kindness

Nakedness of the Moon

An elephant is not separate from his surrounding environment; instead he is an active and integral function within it. The only way forward is to live out the life of an elephant with unquestioning deliberation. His appearance requires neither confirmation nor validation.

It is seldom that an elephant becomes discouraged by the evaluation of others. Just as the moon is not embarrassed by its nakedness when viewed upon from the earth, so it is for the elephant. He belongs here just as he is.

That he is alive is never in question. An elephant participates fully in the experiencing of it. Within him torrents a river of authenticity. He is as he is, and does not seek to be something else.

Just before dawn, a stream gently trickles bedtime stories to the retiring Moon. This is nature's integral language.

A butterfly does not need poetry to express itself.
Its Life is itself an expression of poetry.
That poem is already written
and published in eternity.

We are as much a part of this Universe as are the moons of Jupiter or the rings of Saturn. Within us can be found the elements from far-away galaxies. Surely we walk a sacred path of interconnectedness.

Everything is in Relationship to Everything else

The Moon blushes
and giggles ocean waves
because it is tickled pink
by that warm gravitational
pull toward its old friend
Earth.

Each unfolding moment of the journey can be compared to the experience of an alligator crossing a country highway. The outcome at each crossing is a mystery to us. Our spiritual path involves becoming comfortable with the uncertainty of it.

Each moment of this life is an unrepeatable miracle. If we look deeply into our experience, we will notice that numerous functions are occurring. Thousands of things are going just right to keep us alive in this single moment. Our lives are infinitely precious. It is impossible to apply a value figure upon it. All the gold in the universe could not purchase a ticket for one moment of this journey we are on.

Envision that you are standing atop a high cliff, your feet suddenly slip, and a stranger catches you at the last moment, saving you from certain death. Let's assume this process continues each moment for the next 30 or 40 years. Fairly quickly, we will begin to take things for granted and fail to fully appreciate the stranger's good will actions. After awhile, we may even become critical and resentful regarding the help: "That bastard was rather slow about saving me this time."

With regard to relationship with the Universe, we are innately perfect. We are as much a part of this Universe as are the moons of Jupiter or the rings of Saturn. Within us can be found the elements from far-away galaxies. Surely we walk a sacred path of interconnectedness. We are very much at home on this Earth, without question. We belong.

We cannot consider ourselves to be broken or unworthy, for we are not qualified to evaluate nature's artistry. To be critical of our true nature is like judging a star for twinkling at irregular intervals. Our heart speaks of an obligation to appreciate our aliveness and live fully within each new moment as it unfolds. The terms of agreement lay brightly afront us. Our proper direction is toward the truth of who we are.

'Free As A Bird'

"There is no need to struggle to be free; the ending of the struggle is itself freedom." - Chögyam Trungpa

There is a slogan in Buddhism that goes like this: 'The boundary to what you can accept is the boundary to your freedom'. Often we hear the phrase 'free as a bird' to describe the level of freedom a person has. Let's investigate this phrase, 'free as a bird' to see if there is wisdom to be found within it. A bird is severely restricted by environmental factors and numerous other conditions. A bird is not free... or is he? From another angle of looking at it, a bird is the perfect embodied reflection of freedom itself, because a bird fully accepts the reality of the life he is presented with. You will not often come across a bird that is bitching and squawking about how unfair it is to live out the life of a bird. Human beings, on the other hand, spend much of their lives doing little else.

A human being condemned to a life of incarceration, who fully accepts the reality of the life he has been presented with, is not a prisoner. Instead, he is as 'free as a bird'. True freedom cannot be taken from, or granted to, another person. True freedom is not related to unrestricted movement or action. True freedom is a quality that can be cultivated from within ourselves by practicing acceptance of the reality we are presented with.

Hotel California

There's a song by the Eagles that can be a powerful reflection on the difficulty we have with accepting the reality of life that we are presented with.

A line in the song goes like this: "We are all just prisoners here of our own device". We are always desperately trying to go somewhere else, to that imaginary place where problems don't exist. We create a prison for ourselves through our difficulty with accepting life as it is.

Here's another line: "You can check out anytime you like, but you can never leave." It's true. We can check out using drugs or alcohol or innumerable other methods. We can drift off into fantasy about past and future events. But we can never actually leave. The reality of THIS MOMENT is inescapable.

The way to see sunlight beyond this dark wall of confinement is to practice acceptance of the reality that we are presented with.

Enemy of the People

Many of the problems we face are directly related to our tendency to hold tightly onto narrow views. To think that we have found 'the true path' or 'the right way' reflects a narrow perspective. There is never only one path or one way.

We need to let go of the notion that there can be inflexible answers or solutions. We must look deeply to see beyond any dramatic or judgmental interpretation. We need to be humble enough to learn from mistakes and change direction mid-stream.

Only an open mind can guide us toward positive future outcomes.

A narrow mind is an enemy of the people.

Unliving the Dream...

"Waking up to who you are requires letting go of who you imagine yourself to be"

~Alan Watts

We hear the phrase 'living the dream', but as we walk a path of waking up it might be more accurate to say 'un-living the dream'. This path involves recognizing that we have been conditioned with beliefs and ideas regarding how life should be, and then waking up to the reality of how life actually is. The truth of who we are is far more grand than any stories we may tell ourselves about it.

Love What Is

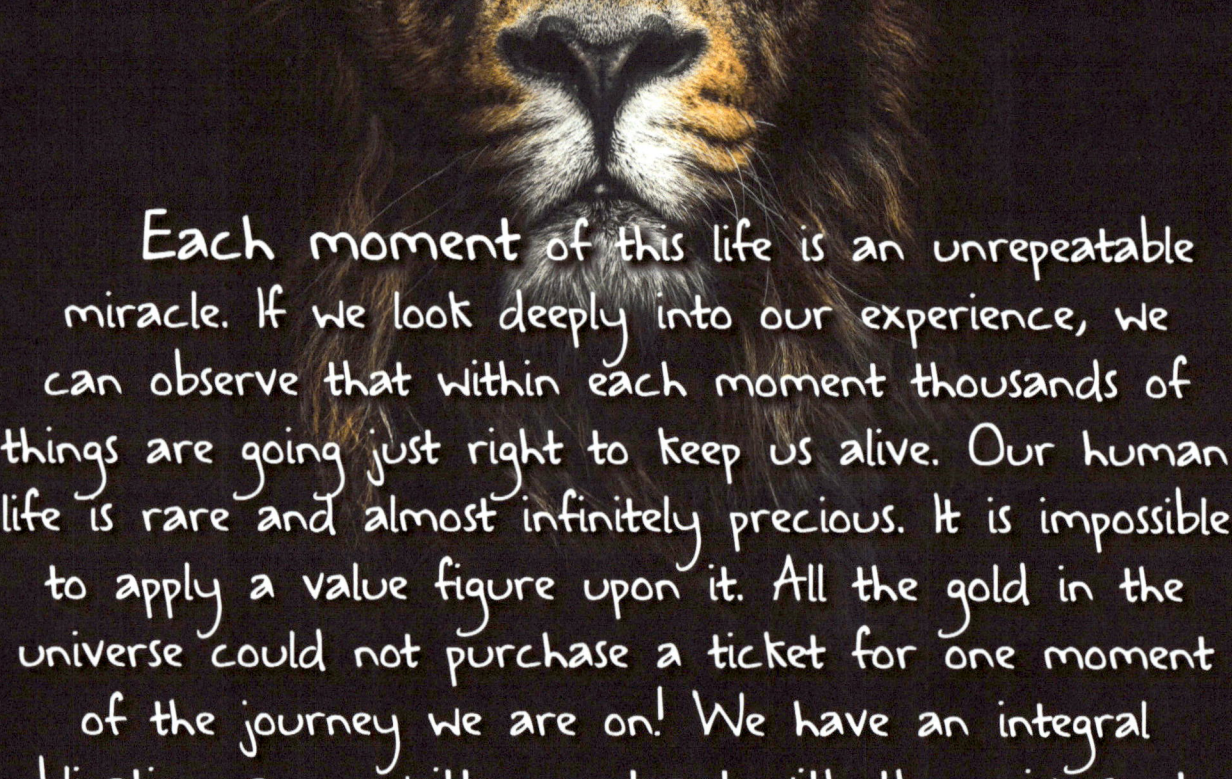

Each moment of this life is an unrepeatable miracle. If we look deeply into our experience, we can observe that within each moment thousands of things are going just right to keep us alive. Our human life is rare and almost infinitely precious. It is impossible to apply a value figure upon it. All the gold in the universe could not purchase a ticket for one moment of the journey we are on! We have an integral obligation, an unwritten contract with the universe, to appreciate our aliveness and to live fully within each new moment as it unfolds. Our path lay brightly afront us. Which way do we go?
Forward!

God, grant me the Serenity to accept the things I cannot change; Courage to change the things I can; and Wisdom to know the difference.
—Serenity Prayer

My friend Rick was a recovering alcoholic with a chronic history. He was diagnosed with cancer and given a time frame within which he could expect to live. When I last met with Rick I asked him how he was able to stay sober through all of this.

"I want to live each day completely during the time I have left" he said quietly. Rick, who was not the spiritual type at all, struck me as being very spiritual that day. He died less than a month after this conversation.

True spirituality engages a powerful ability to live life on life's terms.

We put effort into changing the things that we can change, but then accept the final outcome for what it is. We cooperate with the hand that we are dealt.

There should be a public school class called 'Just Be'.

We live in a world of evolving perspective. Our approach to engaging life is changing from 'doing' to 'being'. We get so caught up in our compulsive 'doing' that we overlook the beauty and mystery that are right here and right now. We forget to 'Just Be'.

What are we 'doing' to acheive? Our true home is this body, this planet, this moment. What is our right way of 'Being' in this world?

That is the question.

Breathing World Peace

"If every 8-year-old in the world is taught meditation, we will eliminate violence from the world within one generation."
~the Dalai Lama

In Buddhist psychology, it is said that all of our possible characteristics exist in the form of seeds in an area called our store consciousness. The seeds of contentment, happiness, and peace can be found here. There are also seeds of anger, violence, divisiveness, and so on. The practice involves watering the seeds we want to blossom and flourish, and not watering the seeds we wish to remain dormant. This process is called selective watering. The seeds of humanity's future can be found within our children. They have not yet blossomed into their full potential. As citizens of the Earth, it is our responsibility to water the correct seeds of mindfulness, compassion, and understanding. If mindfulness were to become a fundamental part of our educational programs, from kindergarten on up, this would have a positive impact on the future of humanity. It could also increase our capacity to peacefully coexist.

"Let your life be your message. Be the change you want to see in the world."
~ Mahatma Gandhi

We create our own happiness, our own misery. We create a world that is peaceful, or one that is plagued with violence. If we want there to be peace in this world, we must first create a peaceful path for ourselves to walk upon. Peace begins with us. Non-violence rests upon a mantle of collective understanding and compassion. If *'I'* can UNDERSTAND that the *'other'* is also suffering, that we are each a product of conditions and life experiences, then violence will cease. Watering the seed of mindfulness in others is a form of social and political activism. World peace is always one collective mindful breath away.

first class?

    I recently helped an elderly woman, who could barely walk, board a commercial airline. She very slowly walked to her assigned seat at the back of the plane, holding on to other seats to help keep her balance. There was a 'First Class' passenger already seated in a perfect spot for this woman. He didn't seem to notice her at all, except that he got up and moved far away to avoid being touched by this person. After she finally walked by, he sat back down and continued reading the newspaper.

    The front seats on a commercial plane should be first occupied by people who need them. If this tradition of 'First Class' is to continue, then those seats should be located toward the back of the plane. And ideally, there should be a sign placed above the 'First Class' area that would read: 'These seats are reserved for people who are shallow and self-absorbed enough to believe that paying more money makes them a better class of human being.'

We cannot consider ourselves to be broken or unworthy, for we are not qualified to evaluate nature's artistry. To be critical of our true nature is like judging a star for twinkling at irregular intervals. Our heart speaks of an obligation to appreciate our aliveness and live fully within each new moment as it unfolds.

Sayeth the fish...

A couple of psychological/spiritual equations. Here is the first:

Stress X Resistance = Increased Suffering

If we don't fully accept our problem, if we deny its existence or divert attention elsewhere, then the problem becomes more problematic.

Here's the second equation:

Stress X Compassionate Present Moment Awareness = Growth, Freedom, Liberation

If while being heartful and fully present we can accept whatever is happening, just as it is, then we can deal with it much more effectively.

Imagine for a moment that you are a fish: the fisherman casts out the line and you take the bait. If you resist and try to quickly swim away, the hook sinks deeper and the severity of your problem is increased. If instead you fully accept your dilemma, make friends with the hook, and swim toward it; if you the fish sayeth to the fisherman, "Thank you sir for providing me with this learning opportunity" - then you may be able to slide up along the curve of the hook and off of it.

We are taught to believe that happiness is contingent upon external conditions and what happens in life, but this is not exactly the true way of things. Happiness is a quality that we can only get to by reaching inward to connect with it. If we seek the world for happiness it cannot be found, because

Happiness is Here Already

Happiness is a pre-existing condition.

What Lies Beneath?

Things look pretty calm on the surface of the Missouri River when you are standing on the bank looking at it... the water moves slowly along. You might think that it is safe to swim there, but appearances can be deceiving. Sometimes there are powerful undercurrents that can pull a person underwater. Many have drowned along the Missouri in just that way. The inner landscape of our mind is like this... lots of undercurrents, eddies, whirlpools, and other powerful unseen forces that can pull us around and affect our emotions and behavior. For the most part, we are only vaguely aware of the hidden process that is working on us virtually all of the time.

Mindfulness is the intentional, accepting, and non-judgmental focus of one's attention on the thoughts, emotions, and sensations that are occurring in the present moment. During mindful practice, we calmly observe all this stuff that comes up in the mind without getting caught up in it. We just observe without forming any opinion; accepting it just as it is. We casually give a name to the thought, emotion, or sensation. Then we let it drift away, like fallen oak leafs resting on river current, without attaching to it. This process can be extremely healing and therapeutic. A psychotherapist would say that we are most profoundly affected by issues that we are only vaguely aware of; issues that are lurking underneath the calm surface.

Here's a quote from psychologist Carl Jung: "Until you make the unconscious conscious, it will direct your life and you will call it fate." Meditation is an explorative excursion into unknown territory. Dark issues that lay beneath begin to brighten and evaporate once positioned under the lamp of awareness.

The little bird spoke with great Clarity, and from that place of Universal Wisdom he had found deep within himself:

"Spirituality is an unfolding experiential process. It is about walking a path toward having our Own experience," he said calmly. "Religion involves sharing in, and believing in, another person's experience."

The woman listened attentively...

'Beginner's Mind'

We have probably all had this experience: A woman is carrying a baby. The baby just stares at you – eyes wide open with awe, wonder, and curiosity. Everything is a brand new experience for this baby. He is not judging you, and has not formed any opinion about you. The baby is not going to suddenly flip you the bird, although we may have seen a horror movie like this once.

What we are looking for in meditation is that PLACE in our perceptual process when we are fully AWARE of our experience, but BEFORE judgements, opinions, and evaluations are formulated. Suzuki Roshi called this PLACE 'Beginner's Mind'. "In the beginner's mind there are many possibilities, but in the expert's there are few."
~Shunryu Suzuki

'Beginner's Mind' is both an attitude we can cultivate and a practice we can use in our meditation. The baby that is staring at you has no idea what to expect; as far as he knows you might suddenly turn into a lizard and fly off into outer space.

"In the beginner's mind there are many possibilities..."

If a person has expansive knowledge of meditation it becomes particularly important that they practice 'Beginner's Mind'.

"...but in the expert's there are few."

Each new moment is unique and unrepeatable. As we walk *THIS PATH in THIS MOMENT*, we are always beginners.

Question:
How many Buddhist psychologists does it take to change a lightbulb?

Answer:
Only one; but FIRST the lightbulb has to be willing to change. SECOND, the psychologist should be prepared to show kindness toward his own injured self in the event that the lightbulb is unwilling to change. THIRD, the psychologist ought to practice Non-attachment to narrow views. He really needs to Let go of this nagging and persistent notion that the lightbulb has to be willing to change. FOURTH, the psychologist ought to practice Acceptance and Non-attachment to outcomes. It may be most appropriate to simply let the lightbulb be just as it is without judging or evaluating it.

A buddhist reflection on the true nature of heaven, purgatory, and hell...

Heaven is when we are enlightened and liberated from suffering

Purgatory is our everyday life: going to school, work, getting married, etc.

Hell is when the remote control to the TV breaks down in such a way that we are forced to watch the Fox News network until the end of time.

We are as much a part of this Universe as are the moons of Jupiter or the rings of Saturn. Within us can be found the elements from far-away galaxies. Surely we walk a sacred path of interconnectedness.

We cannot consider ourselves to be broken or unworthy, for we are not qualified to evaluate nature's artistry. To be critical of our true nature is like judging a star for twinkling at irregular intervals.

We are engaged in a mystery that will never be unraveled

Everything is in Relationship to Everything else.

Everything is Inter-related and Inter-connected.

Everything gets by with a little help from friends.

Everything is in this Together, including Us.

It takes the 'Universe' to make a village.

We Are...

That crisp sound of rustling leaves on a winter night, the trembling first step of a moment-old kitten.

The unspoken word of an ancient prophet, a lingering memory of freedom.

We are all places at all times within life of all variety and persuasion.

An integral function of the limitless equation — without beginning, without end.

We are all form of all measure within all that one day will become.

We are in all things. Look! There we are...

Everything is a piece of the infinitely large and mysterious puzzle. Each piece is necessary to make the puzzle whole and complete.

The little bird spoke with great Clarity, and from that place of Universal Wisdom he had found deep within himself:

"Yes, I know what you mean. We do face many difficulties in this conditioned life," he said softly. "But please keep in mind that you are an integral part of the Universal family. You are as much a part of this Universe as are the moons of Jupiter or the rings of Saturn. Your beginning was forged in the fire of distant and powerful Celestial events. You have the stellar dust from ancient exploded stars coursing through your veins, young lady!"

The woman listened attentively...

Looking to the Moon for answers is a method of self-examination.

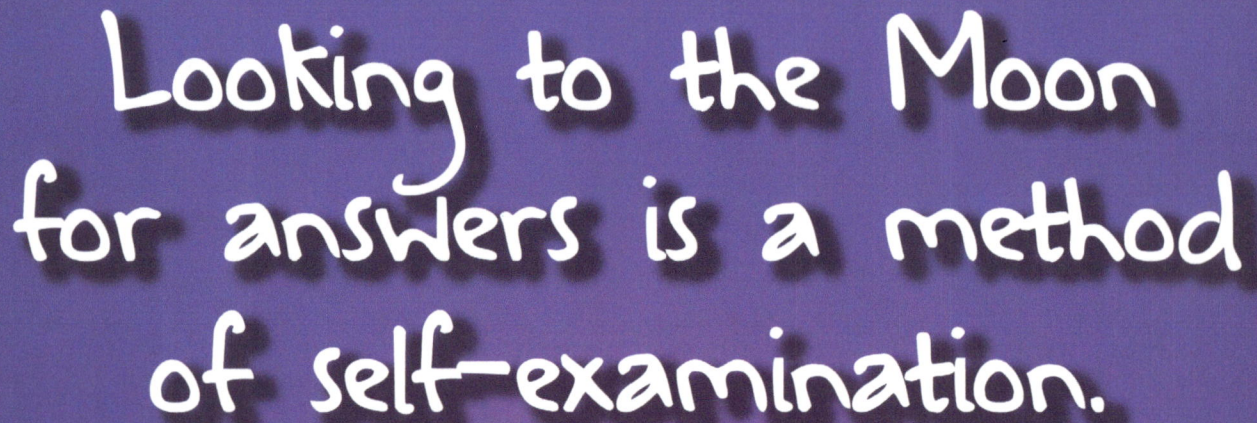

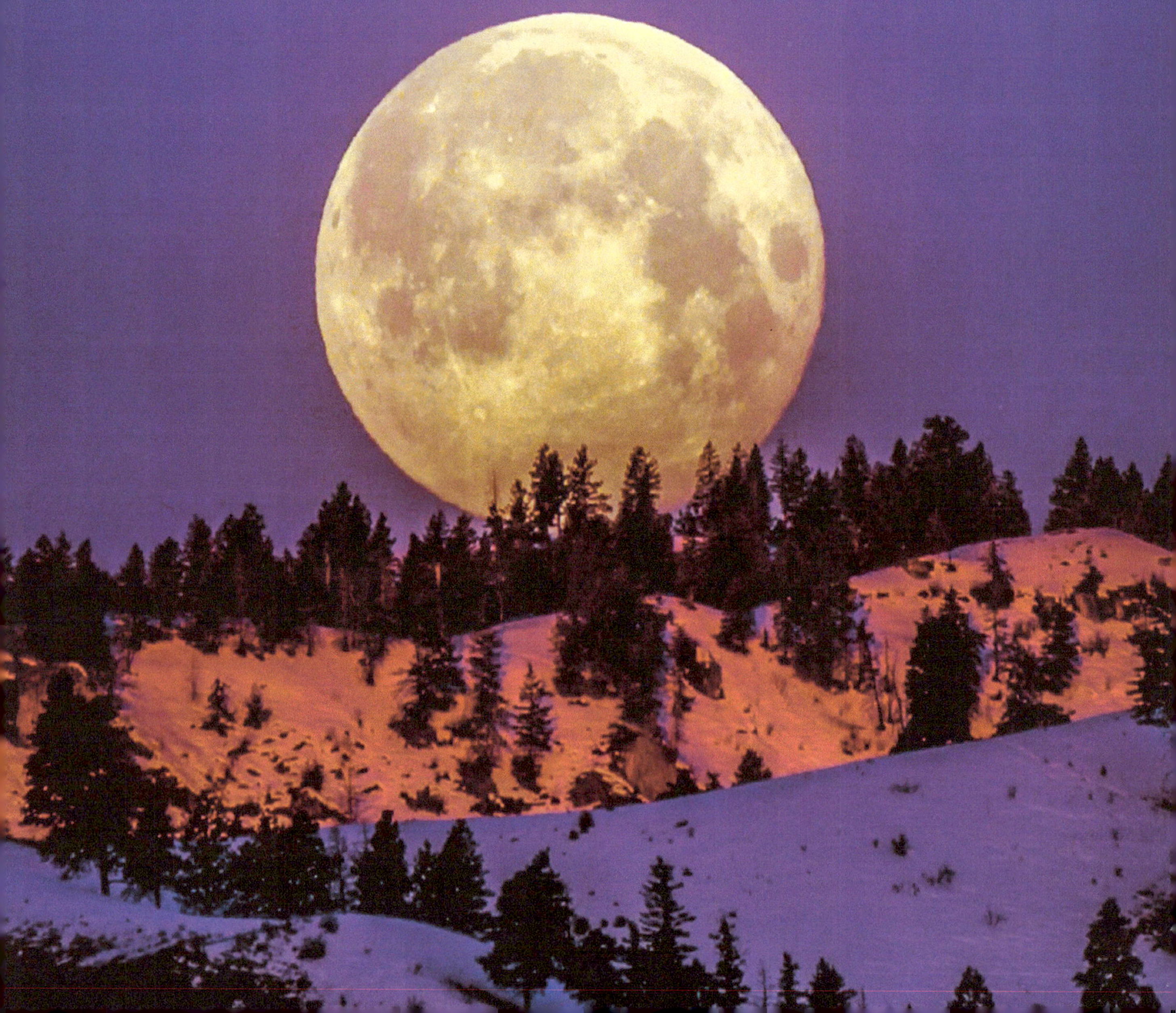

Appreciation

Each moment of this life is an unrepeatable miracle. If we look deeply into our experience, we will notice that numerous functions are occurring. Thousands of things are going just right to keep us alive in this single moment. Our lives are infinitely precious. It is impossible to apply a value figure upon it. All the gold in the universe could not purchase a ticket for one moment of this journey we are on.

Envision that you are standing atop a high cliff, your feet suddenly slip, and a stranger catches you at the last moment, saving you from certain death. Let's assume this process continues each moment for the next 30 or 40 years. Fairly quickly, we will begin to take things for granted and fail to fully appreciate the stranger's good will actions. After awhile, we may even become critical and resentful regarding the help: "That bastard was rather slow about saving me this time."

With regard to relationship with the Universe, we are innately perfect. We are as much a part of this Universe as are the moons of Jupiter or the rings of Saturn. Within us can be found the elements from far-away galaxies. Surely we walk a sacred path of interconnectedness. We are very much at home on this Earth, without question. We belong.

We cannot consider ourselves to be broken or unworthy, for we are not qualified to evaluate nature's artistry. To be critical of our true nature is like judging a star for twinkling at irregular intervals. Our heart speaks of an obligation to appreciate our aliveness and live fully within each new moment as it unfolds. The terms of agreement lay brightly afront us. Our proper direction is toward the truth of who we are.

I would like to thank my loving and supportive family and my beautiful daughter Abigail. A special thank you goes to my brother Kyle Knapp, without whose technical assistance this book would not have been possible. I would also like to to thank: Honey Locust Sangha, First Unitarian Church, and the 48th Street Club for giving me inspiration. The above organizations are located in Omaha, Nebraska USA

Forrest Knapp and daughter Abby

To purchase additional copies of this book or individual full-color posters of Forrest's writings, please visit our website.

www.forrestknapp.com